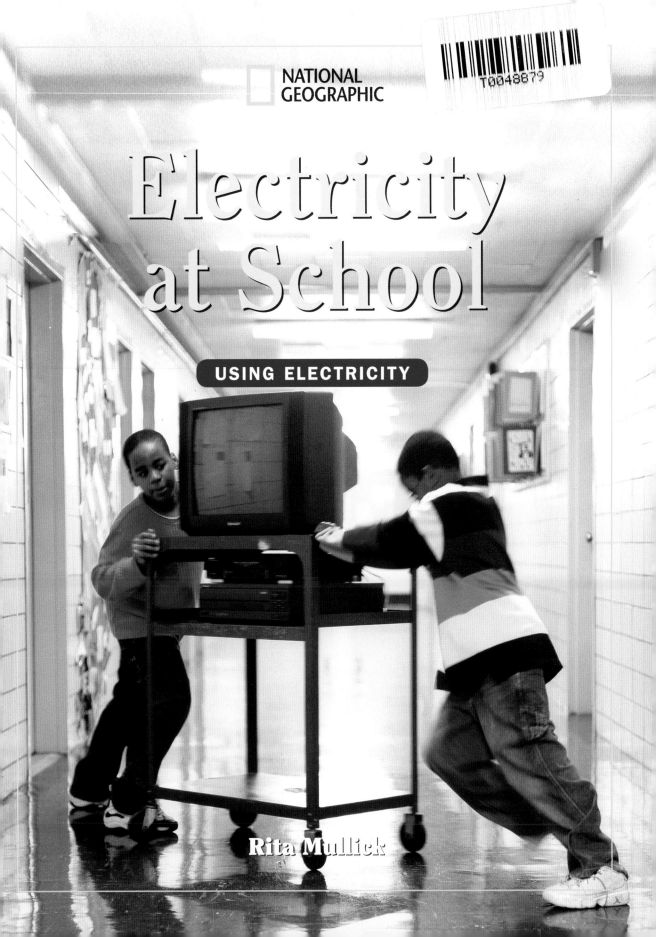

NATIONAL GEOGRAPHIC

Electricity at School

USING ELECTRICITY

Rita Mullick

PICTURE CREDITS

Cover: teenage girl a using microscope in the laboratory © Mel Yates/Taxi/Getty Images.

Page 1 © Photolibrary; page 4 (left), Digital Vision; page 4 (right), Banana Stock; page 5 (top) © Randy Faris/Corbis/Tranz; page 5 (bottom left), Stockdisc Classic; page 5 (bottom right), Emrah Turudu/iStockphoto.com; page 6 © Caroline von Tuempling/Iconica/Getty Images; pages 7–8 © Kevin Currie; page 9 © Macmillan Education Australia; page 11 © Kevin Currie; page 12 © Photolibrary; page 13 (left) © Kevin Currie; page 13 (right), Comstock; page 14 © Stock Central; page 15 © Kevin Currie; page 16 (left), Photodisc; page 16 (middle), shutterstock.com; page 16 (right), Sharon Meredith/iStockphoto.com; page 19 (top), Photodisc; page 19 (middle) © Macmillan Education Australia; page 19 (bottom left) © David Frazier/DanitaDelimont.com; page 19 (bottom second from left) © Ingo Boddenberg/Corbis/Tranz; page 19 (bottom middle) © Photolibrary; page 19 (bottom second from right), Stefan Junger/iStockphoto.com; page 19 (bottom right) © Macmillan Education Australia; pages 21–26 © Alan Laver; page 29, Digital Vision.

Produced through the worldwide resources of the National Geographic Society, John M. Fahey, Jr., President and Chief Executive Officer; Gilbert M. Grosvenor, Chairman of the Board.

PREPARED BY NATIONAL GEOGRAPHIC SCHOOL PUBLISHING
Sheron Long, Chief Executive Officer; Samuel Gesumaria, President; Steve Mico, Executive Vice President and Publisher; Francis Downey, Editor in Chief; Richard Easby, Editorial Manager; Margaret Sidlosky, Director of Design and Illustrations; Jim Hiscott, Design Manager; Cynthia Olson and Ruth Ann Thompson, Art Directors; Matt Wascavage, Director of Publishing Services; Lisa Pergolizzi, Production Manager.

MANUFACTURING AND QUALITY CONTROL
Christopher A. Liedel, Chief Financial Officer; Phillip L. Schlosser, Vice President; Clifton M. Brown III, Director.

EDITOR
Mary Anne Wengel

PROGRAM CONSULTANTS
Dr. Shirley V. Dickson, National Literacy Consultant; James A. Shymansky, E. Desmond Lee Professor of Science Education, University of Missouri-St Louis.

National Geographic Theme Sets program developed by Macmillan Science and Education Australia Pty Limited.

Published by the National Geographic Society
1145 17th Street N.W.
Washington, D.C. 20036-4688

ISBN: 978-1-4263-5157-0

Printed in China by The Central Printing (Hong Kong) Ltd.
Quarry Bay, Hong Kong
Supplier Code: OCP March 2018
Macmillan Job: 804252
Cengage US PO: 15304124

MEA10_Mar18_S

Contents

Using Electricity

Electricity is a form of energy. People use electricity to power many things, from light bulbs to big machines. People use electricity everywhere. They use it at home, at play, at school, and at work.

Key Concepts •••••••••••••••••••••••••••••••••••••••

1. Electricity involves the movement of electrons.
2. An electric circuit is a path along which electrons can move.
3. Electric energy can change to heat, light, sound, and movement.

Where Electricity Is Used

At Home

Appliances at home need electricity to work.

At Play

Some play equipment needs electricity to work.

In this book you will learn how electricity is used at school.

At School

Some school equipment needs electricity to work.

At Work

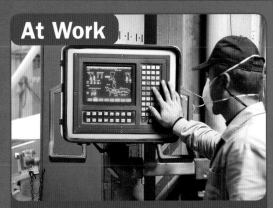

Most office and factory equipment needs electricity to work.

Using Electricity at School

Did you hear a bell ring or use a computer at school today? Did you turn on a light? Did your teacher use an overhead projector? All these things are powered by electricity. If you used any of these things, you used electricity. People at school use electricity in many ways. Can you imagine a world without it?

Key Concept 1 Electricity involves the movement of electrons.

Matter and Atoms

Everything on Earth is made up of matter. Matter is anything that takes up space. All matter is made up of tiny particles called **atoms.** Atoms are very small. You can only see them with the help of a special microscope. A tiny speck of dust contains billions of atoms.

These grains of sand are made up of billions of atoms.

Atoms are made up of even smaller particles. These particles are called protons, neutrons, and **electrons.** Protons and electrons have an **electric charge.** Protons have a positive charge. Electrons have a negative charge. Neutrons do not have any charge. Opposite charges attract each other. This attraction holds protons and electrons together in an atom.

Protons and neutrons make up the center, or nucleus, of an atom. Electrons move around the nucleus.

Parts of an Atom

An electron has a negative charge.

A proton has a positive charge.

Neutron

Nucleus

Electrons and Electricity

The number of electrons and protons in an atom usually remains the same. But electrons can also move from one atom to another. When this happens, an atom gains or loses electrons.

When electrons jump from one atom to another, they push other electrons in front of them. This flow of electrons is called an **electric current.** An electric current carries the energy of moving electrons. This energy is called **electricity.**

*electricity
the energy of
moving electrons*

An electric current flows through wires from one place to another. The electric current reaches your school through wires. At school, people use electricity to power computers, lights, and even filters for fish tanks.

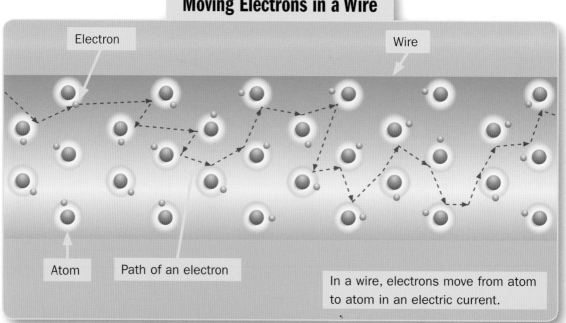

Moving Electrons in a Wire

Electron

Wire

Atom

Path of an electron

In a wire, electrons move from atom to atom in an electric current.

Conductors and Insulators Electrons move easily through materials called **conductors.** The electrons in conductors are loosely connected to their atoms. Some metals are good conductors.

Materials that do not allow electrons to move easily through them are called **insulators.** The electrons in insulators are tightly connected to their atoms. Plastic and rubber are good insulators.

An electric cord is made up of a conductor that is covered with an insulator. The metal wire is the conductor. The plastic covering is the insulator. The insulator makes the cord safe to touch when an electric current is flowing through the wires.

Insulated Wire

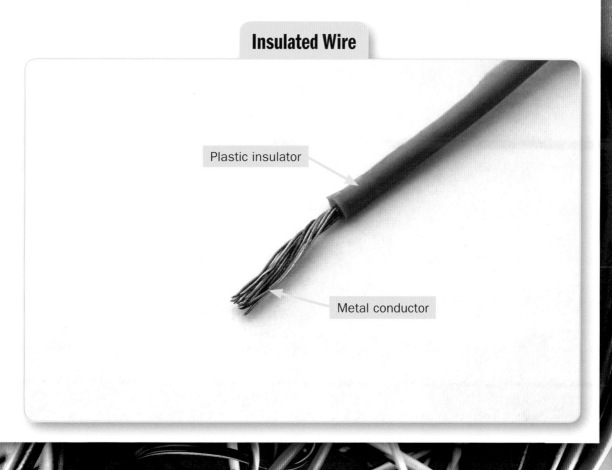

Plastic insulator

Metal conductor

Electric Circuits

Electrons move along a path called an electric **circuit.** Circuits can be closed or open.

circuit

the path along which electrons move

A closed circuit is a complete electric circuit. An open circuit has a gap in it. An electric current can only flow in a closed circuit. Most circuits have a switch. A switch controls the flow of electric current. The switch does this by opening or closing the circuit. In a closed circuit, a current flows from a power source to an electric device and back to the power source.

Some circuits are complex. A complex circuit is made up of many circuits that are connected to one power source.

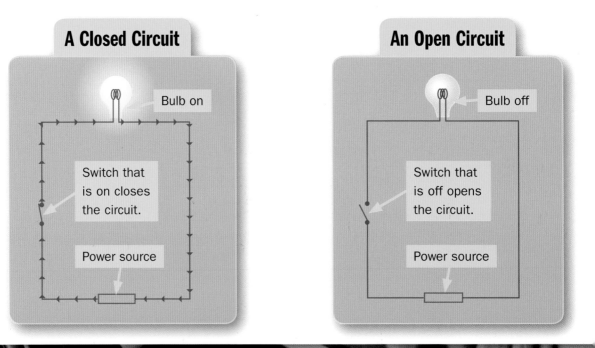

A Closed Circuit

Bulb on

Switch that is on closes the circuit.

Power source

An Open Circuit

Bulb off

Switch that is off opens the circuit.

Power source

The Circuit of Auditorium Floodlights Your school may use floodlights. These lights are part of a circuit. When the power switch for the floodlights is turned on, the electric circuit closes. Closing the circuit makes an electric current flow in a loop. The current flows from the power source through wires to the floodlight bulbs. Electricity lights up the bulbs. Then the current flows from the bulbs through wires back to the power source.

When the power switch is turned off, the circuit opens. This stops the electric current from flowing. The floodlight bulbs do not light up.

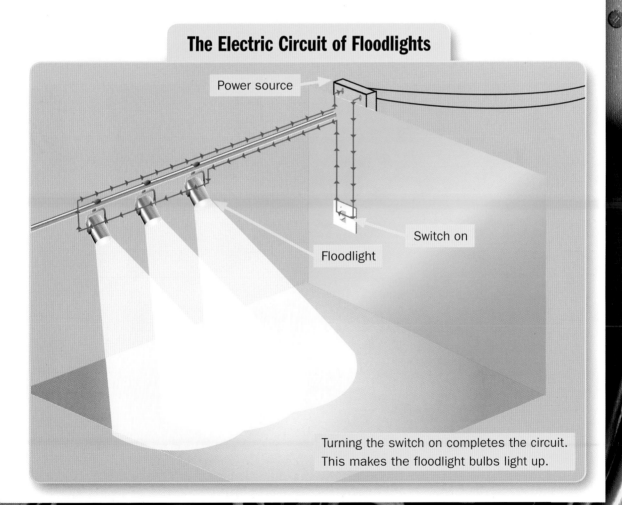

The Electric Circuit of Floodlights

Power source

Switch on

Floodlight

Turning the switch on completes the circuit. This makes the floodlight bulbs light up.

Using Electricity at School

Teachers and students use electricity for many things at school. Electricity enters your school through wires. Different devices in your school change electric energy to other forms of energy, such as heat, light, sound, and movement.

Electric energy can be changed into light to read by. Electric energy powers equipment such as projectors, computers, and the heating or cooling system. It is used in the cafeteria kitchen for heating and cooling the food you eat at lunchtime.

Heating lamps keep food warm in the cafeteria.

Changing Electric Energy to Heat Energy Some devices in a school change electric energy to heat energy. They do this by slowing down the flow of electrons. This is called **resistance.** Resistance in a material slows down the flow of electric current. Slowing down the flow of electric current causes electrons to collide with each other as they move. When electrons collide, they produce heat.

The water heater at your school provides hot water. The water heater heats water that is used in bathrooms. To do this, an electric current flows through a circuit from the power source to an **element** inside the heater. The element has high resistance. It becomes hot when the electric current flows through it. Water passing through the water heater is warmed by the heat from the element.

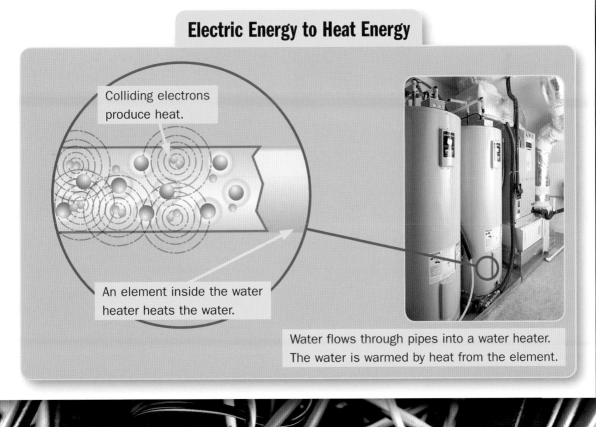

Electric Energy to Heat Energy

Colliding electrons produce heat.

An element inside the water heater heats the water.

Water flows through pipes into a water heater. The water is warmed by heat from the element.

Changing Electric Energy to Light Energy Some devices change electric energy to light energy. Light bulbs and lights in overhead projectors are devices that do this.

The light in an overhead projector has a thin wire inside it. The thin wire is called a **filament.** When the projector switch is turned on, an electric current moves from the power source to the filament. The filament has high resistance. It heats up when the electric current flows through it. The heat makes the filament glow and give off light. Light filaments are made from a metal called tungsten. Tungsten can withstand very high temperatures without melting.

An overhead projector changes electric energy to light energy.

Changing Electric Energy to Sound Energy Some devices change electric energy to sound energy. Your school bell uses electric energy to make sound. The bell has an **electromagnet.** The electromagnet becomes a magnet when an electric current flows through it. The bell also has a movable metal part attached to a clapper.

Pressing the school bell completes the bell's circuit. It makes the electromagnet active. The electromagnet attracts the metal part. When the metal part moves, the clapper attached to it moves too. The clapper hits the bell and makes a sound. The movement of the metal part breaks the circuit. The electromagnet loses its **magnetism** and the metal part and clapper spring back. This completes the circuit again. The process repeats very quickly. This produces a constant ringing sound.

How an Electric School Bell Works

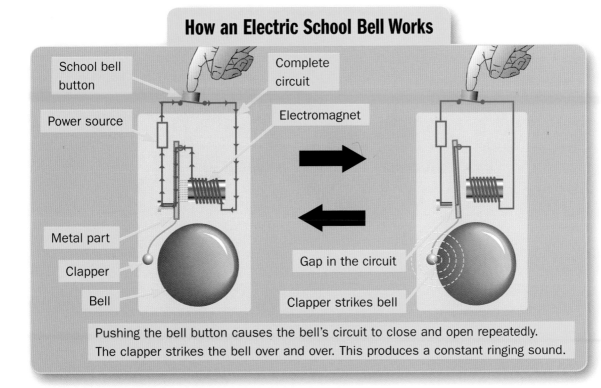

School bell button

Complete circuit

Power source

Electromagnet

Metal part

Clapper

Bell

Gap in the circuit

Clapper strikes bell

Pushing the bell button causes the bell's circuit to close and open repeatedly. The clapper strikes the bell over and over. This produces a constant ringing sound.

Changing Electric Energy to Movement Some devices change electric energy to movement, or **mechanical energy.** Mechanical energy can be used to do work. A device that changes electric energy to mechanical energy usually has a part called a motor. Different motors do different jobs. Motors are found in fans, floor polishers, and elevators at your school.

An electric motor has magnets that attract and repel each other when an electric current flows into it. The motor in a fan changes electric energy to mechanical energy. This is used to rotate the fan blades. The rotating blades cool the air in a room by swirling the air around.

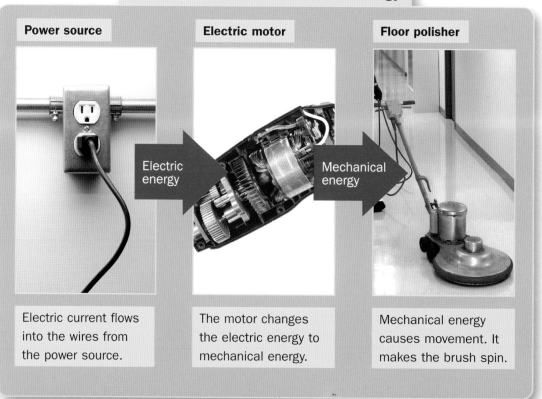

Electric Energy to Mechanical Energy

Power source

Electric motor

Floor polisher

Electric energy

Mechanical energy

Electric current flows into the wires from the power source.

The motor changes the electric energy to mechanical energy.

Mechanical energy causes movement. It makes the brush spin.

Think About the Key Concepts

Think about what you read. Think about the pictures and diagrams. Use them to answer the questions. Share what you think with others.

1. What is electricity? What do electrons have to do with electricity?

2. How are conductors and insulators used together?

3. What does a switch do in an electric circuit?

4. What other forms of energy can electric energy change to?

Flow Diagram

Diagrams use pictures and words to explain ideas.
You can learn new ideas without having to read a lot of words.

There are different kinds of diagrams.
The diagram on page 19 is a flow diagram. It shows how electricity gets to a school. A flow diagram uses pictures and captions to show how something takes place. It shows the steps in a process. Look back at the diagram on page 16. It is a flow diagram of how electric energy changes to mechanical energy.

How to Read a Diagram

1. **Read the title.**
   It tells you what the diagram is about.

2. **Read the labels or captions.**
   They tell you about the parts of the diagram.

3. **Study the pictures.**
   Pictures help show the steps. The arrows are pictures too. They show the order of the steps.

4. **Think about what you learned.**
   Decide what new information you learned from the diagram.

From the Power Station to the School

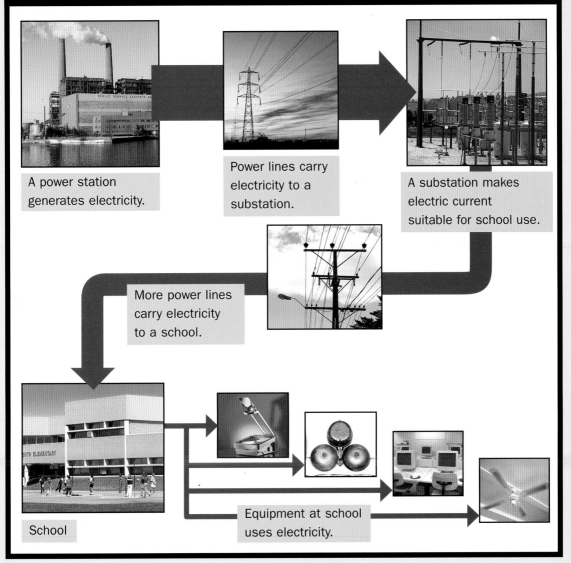

A power station generates electricity.

Power lines carry electricity to a substation.

A substation makes electric current suitable for school use.

More power lines carry electricity to a school.

School

Equipment at school uses electricity.

Follow the Arrows

Read the diagram by following the steps on page 18. Write down what you learned about how electricity gets to a school. Where is electricity generated? What does electricity flow through? How is electricity used at school? Explain the process to a classmate.

How-to Books

The purpose of **how-to books** is to give directions. How-to books take many forms.

Cookbook

Craft Book

Exercise Manual

How to...

How-to Books

User Manual

Gardening Guide

You use different how-to books to find out how to make or do something. If you want to know how to use a machine, you read a user manual. User manuals come with machines when you buy them.

User manuals give you all the information you need to know before you use a machine. They tell you how to operate the machine. They also tell you how to care for the machine and how to use it safely.

Overhead Projector User Manual

The **title** tells which machine the user manual is for.

Congratulations on buying a new overhead projector. Read the information in this user manual before using your overhead projector. This manual will tell you how to use and take care of your overhead projector.

Parts of the Overhead Projector

Subheads break the information into easy-to-find sections.

A Mirror lift tab

B Projection mirror

C Head release button

D Support

E Power cord

F Support lock

G Support cradle latch

H Folding-leg release latch

I Power switch

J Stage glass

K Focus knob

Labels show the parts of the machine.

Diagrams show in pictures what the information means.

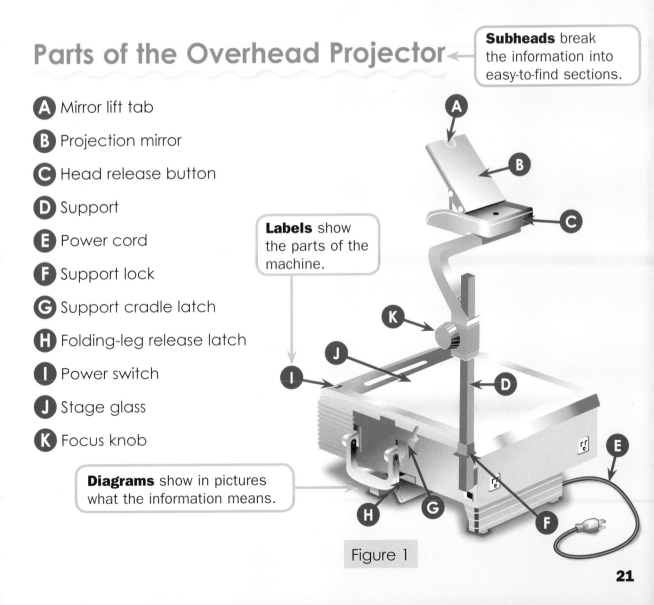

Figure 1

Safety Measures

When using your overhead projector, always follow basic safety measures.

⚠ Read and understand all instructions before using your overhead projector.

⚠ Do not expose the overhead projector to direct sunlight. Sunlight can damage the projector. (Figure 2)

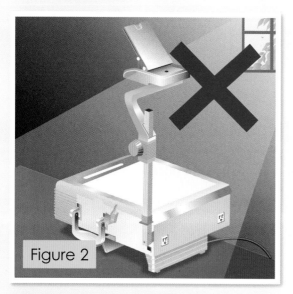

Figure 2

⚠ Do not operate the projector if the power cord is damaged. Call a trained technician to check it for you.

⚠ Never immerse the overhead projector in water.

⚠ Keep the overhead projector out of reach of young children.

⚠ Do not leave the projector unattended while it is in use.

⚠ Do not leave the power cord where someone can trip over it. (Figure 3)

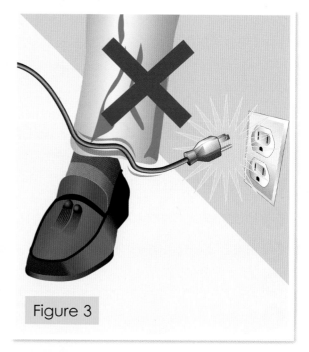

Figure 3

Important information is presented in bulleted lists so it is easy to find and read.

Setting Up the Overhead Projector

This overhead projector can enlarge and display notes, diagrams, and photographs. The projector projects images onto a wall or screen. It is a useful tool for classroom lessons and for making presentations.

- Place the projector on a table or other flat surface.

- Lift up both folding-leg release latches to unfold legs. (Figure 4) The lamp will not light up unless the folding legs are down.

- Release the support cradle latch. Then lift the support to an upright position. (Figure 5)

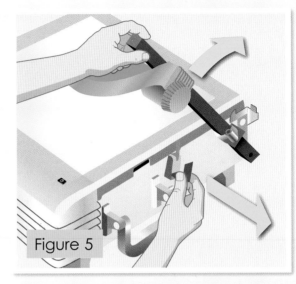

Figure 5

- Push the head release button and rotate it till it locks into place. (Figure 6)

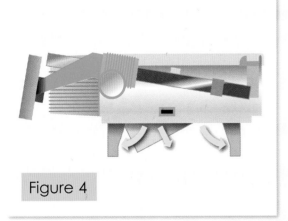

Figure 4

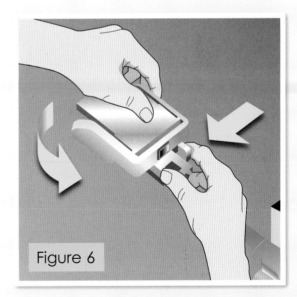

Figure 6

- Hold the mirror lift tab and lift up the projection mirror.

Using the Overhead Projector

- Place the overhead projector in front of a screen or white wall. The distance from the screen controls the size of the projected image.

- Plug the power cord into the power source. (Figure 7)

Figure 7

- Push the projector's power switch to light up the lamp.

- Rotate the projector until the light beam is in line with the screen or wall. (Figure 8)

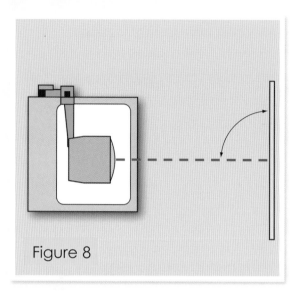

Figure 8

- Adjust the angle of the projection mirror to raise or lower the image on the screen.

- Rotate the focus knob to get the clearest image.

Troubleshooting

Use this section to solve any problems with the overhead projector.

The Overhead Projector Does Not Work

- Make sure the projector is plugged in correctly.

- Check that the light bulb is working and has not burned out.

- If the light bulb has burned out, replace it with a new one.

Replacing the Light Bulb

- Make sure you replace the light bulb with the correct bulb for your overhead projector.

- Turn off the projector. Unplug it from the power source.

- Release the cover latch and lift up the cover.

- Remove the light bulb.

- Push the new light bulb fully into the socket. (Figure 9)

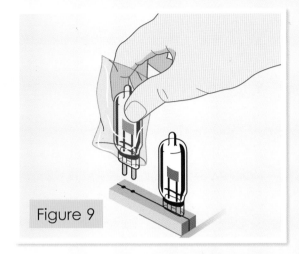

Figure 9

- Close the cover, plug in the power cord, and turn on the projector.

A New Light Bulb Fails

- Make sure the new light bulb is fitted correctly.

The Projected Image Is Dim

- Check the stage glass and mirror for dust or dirt.

- Adjust the light bulb and make sure it is fitted correctly.

If the overhead projector still does not work properly, turn it off and consult a technician.

Caring for the Overhead Projector

Placement

- Do not place the overhead projector on a slanted surface. It may fall.

- Do not use the overhead projector in places where it is too hot or too cold. (Figure 10)

- Always keep your overhead projector in a place free of dust, dirt, and moisture.

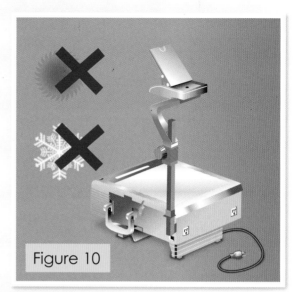

Figure 10

Cleaning

- Always unplug the overhead projector before cleaning it.

- Let the projector cool completely before moving it.

- Use a soft, dry cloth to dust the stage glass and base.

- Do not wipe the projection mirror. Use a soft brush to remove dust from it. (Figure 11)

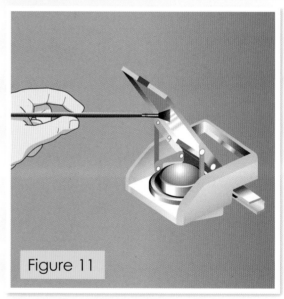

Figure 11

Apply the Key Concepts

Key Concept 1 Electricity involves the movement of electrons.

Activity

Think about what you know about electrons. What are electrons? Can you see electrons with your eyes? What do electrons have to do with electricity? Draw a word web showing what you know about electrons.

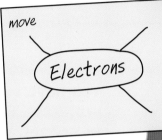

Key Concept 2 An electric circuit is a path along which electrons can move.

Activity

Look around you. Name four objects that are part of an electric circuit. Choose one and draw a circuit for that object. Label the parts of the circuit.

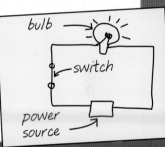

Key Concept 3 Electric energy can change to heat, light, sound, and movement.

Activity

Write a paragraph or two about something you used today that uses electricity. Did it change electric energy into another kind of energy? How was that useful to you?

I turned on the TV....

Write Your Own User Manual

You have read the user manual for the overhead projector. Now think of a different machine you use at school. Write a user manual for it.

1. Study the Model

Look back at the user manual on pages 21–26. What information is presented under each section? How do bulleted lists make the information easy to find and read? How do diagrams help you understand the information in the user manual?

2. Choose a Machine

Choose a machine you use at school. Make notes on what the machine does and how it operates. Think about how it should be used safely. How should you clean and take care of the machine? What should you do if something goes wrong with the machine?

User Manual

- Break the information into easy-to-find sections.
- Present the information in bulleted lists.
- Use diagrams to support the text.
- Include important safety measures.

3. Write a User Manual

Use subheads that are similar to the ones in the overhead projector user manual. Present the important information clearly in bulleted lists under the subheads. Try to make your information and instructions easy to follow and understand.

4. Draw Diagrams

Draw a diagram and label the different parts of your machine. Then draw smaller diagrams to help illustrate the information in your bulleted lists.

5. Read over Your Work

Read over your user manual, correcting any spelling mistakes or punctuation errors. Make sure your user manual is easy to understand. Are your instructions for use easy to follow? Do your diagrams clearly illustrate the text? Have you listed all the safety measures? Did you describe how to care for the machine? Is there any other information the user of the machine might need to know?

Safety Measures

- Never use the machine near water.

- Unplug the machine after use.

- Keep the machine out of the reach of children.

Present Your User Manual

Now that you have chosen a machine and written a user manual for it, you can present your user manual to the rest of the class.

How to Present Your User Manual

1. **Copy your labeled diagram onto an overhead transparency.**
   Draw the diagram clearly so you can show the different parts of your machine to the class.

2. **Explain your machine to the class.**
   Take turns presenting your machines in class. Show the class the different parts of your machine on the overhead projector. Explain to the class what the machine is used for and how the machine works.

3. **Explain the safety measures.**
   It is important to follow the safety measures carefully when you use any machine. Tell the class of any possible dangers with using your machine. Explain how to use the machine in the safest way possible.

4. **Show the class how to care for the machine.**
   Tell the class how to clean, store, and care for the parts of your machine to keep it in the best working order.

Glossary

atoms – tiny particles that make up matter

circuit – the path along which electrons move

conductors – materials through which an electric current moves easily

electric charge – a property within an electron or a proton. A charge may be positive or negative.

electric current – the movement of electrons

electricity – the energy of moving electrons

electromagnet – a piece of metal that becomes a magnet when an electric current passes through a wire wound around it

electrons – particles that move around the center of an atom

element – a metal part that heats quickly when an electric current passes through it

filament – a wire that glows when heated by an electric current

insulators – materials through which an electric current moves with difficulty

magnetism – force that attracts or repels

mechanical energy – the energy of movement or moving parts

resistance – slowing down the flow of electrons

Index